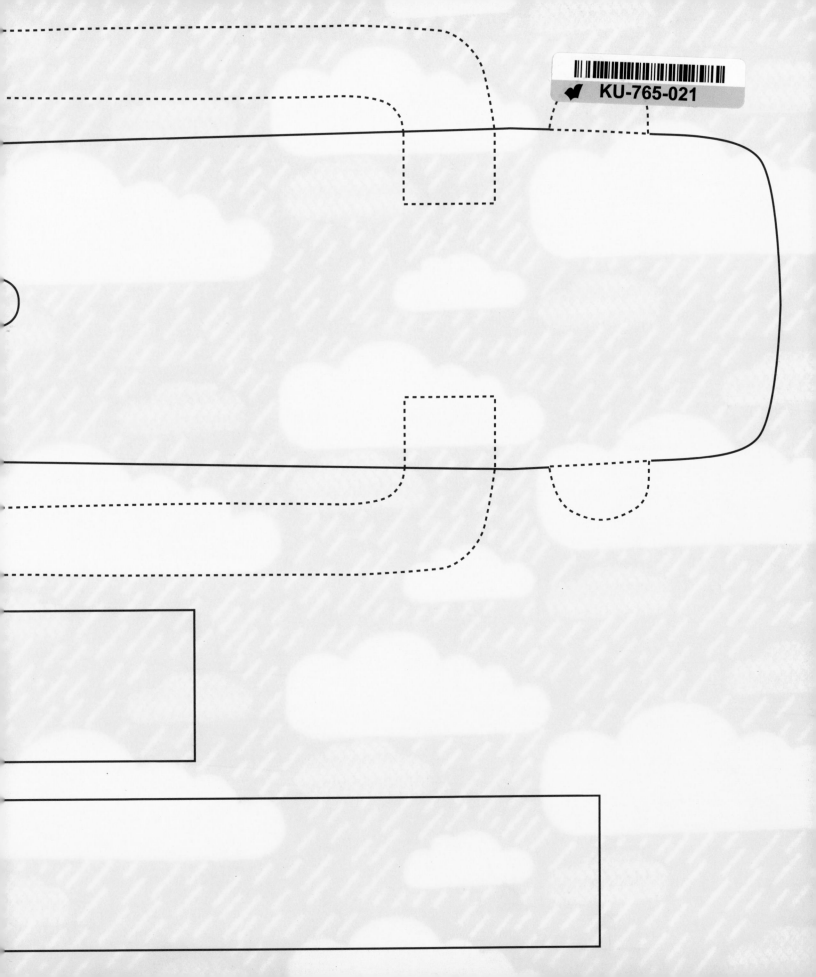

creative creatures

KINGFISHER

SPECIAL THANKS:
I would like to thank my grandma,
Laura Wilson, for encouraging me to be creative
from an early age and for being a great teacher.
I'd also like to thank Kate Beckett, Elaine Gann
and Erin McIntyre for their creativity and help
with making the props and creatures in
this book, and Gareth for making the
photoshoot such fun.

KINGFISHER

First published 2013 by Kingfisher
an imprint of Macmillan Children's Books
a division of Macmillan Publishers Limited
20 New Wharf Road, London N1 9RR
Basingstoke and Oxford
Associated companies throughout the world
www.panmacmillan.com

Design: Jo Connor   Editor: Carron Brown
Photography: Gareth Hacker

ISBN 978-0-7534-3541-0

Copyright © Donna Wilson 2013

1 3 5 7 9 8 6 4 2
1TR/1012/WKT/UG/140MFO

A CIP catalogue record for this book is available
from the British Library.

Printed in China

Contents

Start creating

Donna Wilson was named Designer of the Year at the British Design Awards in 2010. She set up her own company in 2003 after making knitted creatures at the Royal College of Art, London. The hand-made creatures and an ever-expanding range of products for the home are now sold all around the world.

If you've ever wondered what your cuddly toys do when you're not in the room, this book will give you an idea. Ralf and Rill create a tidier-upper robot, Olive Owl designs an owl kite and Cyril makes a sleeping Charlie Monkey doll. As well as fun friends, there are practical projects, such as a draught excluder, a mobile phone cosy and something to do with odd socks. Follow the creatures' step-by-step instructions and create until your heart's content.

Sewing tips

You don't have to be a great stitcher to make these projects. To begin sewing, you either tie a knot in the end of the thread, or you can make a holding stitch – a stitch that you stitch over three or four times. I use a piece of thread doubled to make it stronger. Make sure it's not too long or you might get in a tangle. Always be careful when using a needle.

I used an over stitch on the Charlie doll's arm (see page 45), and all round the sausage dog draught excluder (see page 29). Your over stitching will be seen, but if you do small, close-together stitching, it will look nice and neat.

OVER STITCH

Go over the two edges of the fabric.

Needle pushes through from one fabric edge to the other

Needle pushes through the two layers of fabric at the same time.

RUNNING STITCH

Runs along the length of the fabric in small stitches.

I use a running stitch a lot. It's a quick way to sew two pieces of fabric together. Normally I sew round a shape then turn it inside out so the stitches are hidden. Make the stitches small and close together so gaps can't be seen when the shape is stuffed.

When you see the word 'embroider', this means to decorate with stitching.

5

Mitten Kitten's play

Big Ted

Mitten Kitten

Mitten Kitten loves to sing, but her friends just can't stand her high-pitched voice. They always tell her to stop. So, instead, Mitten Kitten decided to direct her very own play. She cast two of her favourite characters, Wilbur and Big Ted, as the lead actors.

Mitten wrote a musical and the pair had to sing, dance and act – all at the same time! "Let's have a dress rehearsal. Action!" shouted Mitten, who was very excited.

Wilbur was a little nervous at first, but he plucked up all his courage and performed in his loudest, deepest voice. Big Ted had all the moves as he danced round the stage kicking his long legs. They both put on a fantastic performance, and didn't even forget any of their lines. Mitten Kitten was so proud – her story had come to life!

Wilbur

6

Rill

Ralf and Rill love playing games and love playing tricks on each other even more. One day, they decided to go for a walk together.

"I'll race you to the hilltop!" shouted Ralf, and he scampered off before Rill could catch his breath. Rill trotted after him, but he couldn't catch up. "I'll race you to the treetop," chirped Ralf, and he leapt from branch to branch. Rill was close on his heels, but he still couldn't keep up. "I'll race you back down!" shouted Ralf. "Wheeeeeeee!" he squealed, as he swung to the ground, snapping twigs as he went. Rill flew down the trunk, but still he was too slow.

"I'll race you down the hill!" shouted Ralf. Suddenly, Rill spotted one of Charlie's old banana skins. He jumped on it and with a huge whoosh he slid so fast on the slithery, slippery skin that he overtook Ralf and was first to the bottom of the hill!

Ralf

Ralf and Rill's slidey race

Ralf and Rill's sock monster

The situation in the sock drawer has got out of hand. There are socks everywhere! Ralf and Rill decided to make a sock monster to sort things out.

Your sock monster can have any number of arms and different coloured claws.

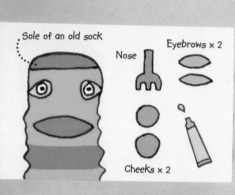

Cut out pieces of felt for the cheeks, eyelids, eyebrows and nose, and either glue or sew them into place on the sole part of an old sock. For added monster madness, stick on plastic googly eyes.

Now you've made one sock monster, try making him some sock creature friends.

What you will need
• coloured felt • scissors • old sock • glue •
• needle and thread • plastic googly eyes •
• fabric • pipe cleaners •

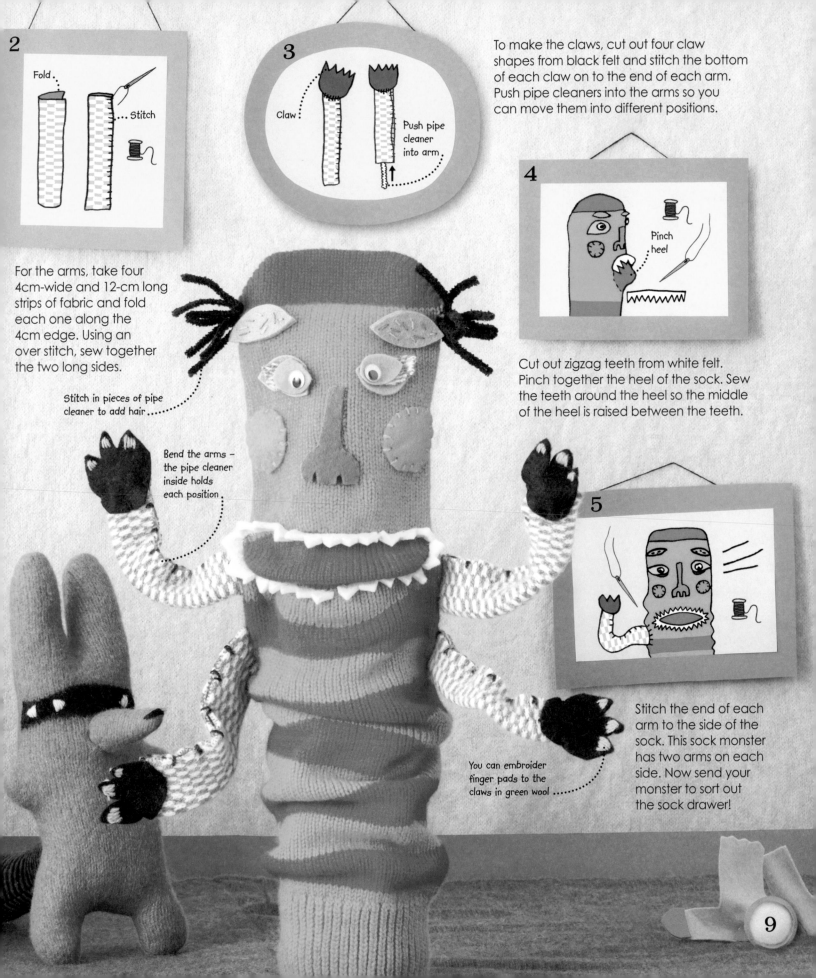

2

Fold

Stitch

3

Claw

Push pipe cleaner into arm

To make the claws, cut out four claw shapes from black felt and stitch the bottom of each claw on to the end of each arm. Push pipe cleaners into the arms so you can move them into different positions.

4

Pinch heel

For the arms, take four 4cm-wide and 12-cm long strips of fabric and fold each one along the 4cm edge. Using an over stitch, sew together the two long sides.

Cut out zigzag teeth from white felt. Pinch together the heel of the sock. Sew the teeth around the heel so the middle of the heel is raised between the teeth.

Stitch in pieces of pipe cleaner to add hair

Bend the arms – the pipe cleaner inside holds each position

5

Stitch the end of each arm to the side of the sock. This sock monster has two arms on each side. Now send your monster to sort out the sock drawer!

You can embroider finger pads to the claws in green wool

Olive Owl's kite

It was a windy day and Olive needed
a friend to fly with. So she decided to make
an owl kite from tissue paper and wire.

Tape the sharp
ends together.

1

Using pliers, bend a thin wire into an
owl shape. Carefully tape the sharp
ends together to complete the shape.
Add a wire crossbar. Secure the centre
and sides of the bar with sticky tape.

Bend each end of the
crossbar back on itself to
form a hook around the edge.

2

Cut out a layer of tissue paper
1cm larger than your kite frame.
Snip small cuts about 1cm apart all
around the frame to form small flaps.

Be careful
not to rip the
tissue paper.

Glue on triangles
of different coloured
tissue paper to
give your kite a
feathery pattern.

5

Knot one end of string tightly around a thick piece of card. Wind the rest of the string around the card. Tie the other end of the string around the centre of the crossbar. Your kite is ready to fly!

Card

4

Cut out shapes from different coloured tissue paper to make your owl's eyes, beak, wings, tail and feathers. Glue these on to the front of the kite.

3

Fold and stick flaps

Fold each small flap over the wire frame and glue it down carefully. Some flaps might overlap, but that is fine.

What you will need

• pliers • thin wire, around 0.5mm thick •
• sticky tape • different colours of tissue paper •
• scissors • clear-drying glue •
• string (6m long) • thick card •

Cyril's pop-up card

Cyril wanted to surprise Charlie to say 'Thank You' for the party Charlie had given him. A pop-up card will do the trick!

1 Fold a piece of yellow A4 card in the middle and open it out. Decorate the bottom of the card with green and blue hills cut out of paper or card.

Hill shapes are a good way to create a landscape

Add your message on white speech bubbles.

2 Trace the nose template (see page 48) on to orange card. Cut out the shape and fold over the two tabs.

3 Roll into a cone

Shape the Cyril nose into a cone. Stick the cone together along the long edge with tape. Mark the tip of the nose in pen.

Add a black nose

What you will need
• yellow A4 card • blue, green and white paper or card • scissors • glue • sticky tape • pencil • • tracing paper • orange card • black pen •

4 Slits

Fold

On orange card, draw a Cyril shape that's 24cm from ear tip to lower body. Fold Cyril in two lengthways. Make a slit at either side of the fold above the arms. Insert the nose tabs into the slits and secure the tabs with sticky tape.

Secure tabs on the back with sticky tape

5 Glue Cyril in the middle of the A4 card along the fold, with the two ears sticking out of the top. Stick down the eyes (white card with black pen pupils). Fold the card and then open it – the nose will pop out in glorious 3D!

Draw Cyril's furry chest with a pen

13

Mitten Kitten's phone cosy

Mitten Kitten is always on the go, organizing things. Her phone is in constant use. She needs a phone cosy to keep it safe.

How about...?

To give your phone cosy extra special style, you might want to use two different fabrics — one pattern for the outside and another colour for the inner lining.

1

1cm gap

1cm gap

1cm gap

Double the width of your phone

Find two pieces of coloured or patterned fabric. Lay one on top of the other and pin at the corners. Lay the phone on top of the layers. Cut the fabric so it's double the width of the phone and 1cm larger at the top, bottom and left-hand side.

Once inside its cosy, your phone will be less likely to be scratched by claws or other sharp things.

2

Sew together along the bottom edge......

Open out

Sewn edge......

Pin together the two fabrics. Sew them together along the bottom edge. Open out the fabric so the sewn edge is in the centre.

Fold up the opened-out fabric along the longest edge with the seam on the inside. Pin together the corners and sew the fabric together along the longest edge, forming a tube.

3

The seam (the neat join between the two fabrics) is on the inside......

Sew together along the longest edge......

4

Lining fabric ......

Outer fabric ......

Turn the tube so that the longest seam is at the centre, running top to bottom. The lining fabric is the top half of the tube and the outer fabric is the bottom half.

What you will need
• fabric, such as from an old jumper •
• ruler • pen • scissors • pins •
• needle and thread • felt • glue •

How about...?

Stitch a ribbon or other long piece of material to either side of the phone cosy so you can hang it around your neck.

Sew along the bottom edge of the tube. Turn the sealed tube inside out so it's the right way round, with the seams on the outside.

6

Tuck the lining into the outer fabric ....

Lining fabric...

Sew together the open edges of the lining fabric and push the lining right down to the bottom of the outer fabric pocket to create the body of the cosy.

5

Sew here..

Your phone will fit snugly into its cosy.

7

Cut out triangular ears from felt and sew or glue them to the top of the outer layer. For the eyes, cut two white ovals from felt and sew or glue two black pupils in the centre of each eye. Sew or stick the eyes below the ears.

With a needle and black thread embroider lines for the nose and mouth. Stitch on long threads for whiskers. Your phone cosy is now ready to travel!

Embroider a nose and mouth using black thread

8

You could also make a cosy for a book or an MP3 player.

What you will need

- old glove • polyester toy stuffing •
- needle and thread •
- felt • scissors • wool •
- small pom-pom •

If you can't find polyester toy stuffing, you can use the stuffing out of an old cushion or pillow.

Mitten Kitten's whiskers are stitched-on woolly threads....

Big Ted and Wilbur's Mitten Kitten

Odd socks and odd gloves can be made into new friends! Wilbur and Big Ted found an old glove and made their own Mitten Kitten.

18

1

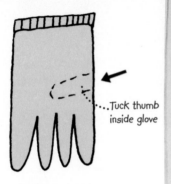

...Tuck thumb inside glove

Find an old glove – one that has lost its partner and is not worn any more. Tuck the thumb inside the body of the glove.

2

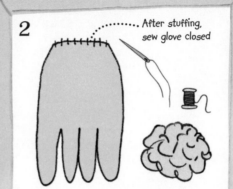

After stuffing, sew glove closed

Stuff the glove with polyester toy stuffing, making sure the stuffing goes into all the fingers. Seal the stuffing by sewing together the open end of the glove.

3

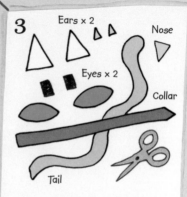

Ears x 2   Nose

Eyes x 2

Collar

Tail

Cut out felt shapes: triangles for the ears, a triangle for the nose, ovals and rectangles for the eyes, and two long pieces for the collar and tail.

4

Using an over stitch, attach the tail on to the stuffed glove where the thumb used to be.

5

Embroider the mouth with black thread and stitch on the ears, nose and eyes. Stitch on some wool to make whiskers.

6

Wrap the collar around her neck and cut it to fit. Secure the collar by stitching it to the body. Add a small pom-pom as a bell.

Your Mitten Kitten doll can have a tail of any colour or pattern.

How about...?

Instead of a pom-pom bell, make a name tag from a piece of yellow or grey felt and embroider a name (perhaps M. K. – Mitten Kitten's initials).

Big Ted and Wilbur's creation

Big
Ted

Wilbur

Big Ted and Wilbur are both very good at making things, but they never ever like cleaning up the mess they create. "I have an idea," squealed Wilbur excitedly. "Why don't we make a tidier-upper robot so we never have to clean!" "What a fantastic plan!" agreed Big Ted.

The pair immediately began searching for materials to make the super tidier-upper robot. Wilbur emptied the kitchen cupboards, and found tin foil and bottle tops for the robot's switches. Big Ted trawled through the shed, finding all sorts of cardboard tubes and boxes for the robot's body.

They stuck their found materials together and soon the robot took shape. When Wilbur pressed the 'On' switch, the robot's eyes opened... he took a step forward... "Give me your command," said the robot. Big Ted looked around at the mess they had made. "Tidy up, robot!" he commanded. The robot swivelled his head, looked around, then switched himself off and began to snore. Wilbur and Big Ted had created a robot that didn't like tidying either!

Cyril

Charlie

Cyril's great adventure

Charlie

Cyril Squirrel-fox's great-grandfather was a famous explorer. He discovered the tallest oak tree in the giant acorn forest. He was also the first to capture a wild wolf using only his quick wit and survival skills.

Cyril felt he could never be as brave or adventurous as his great-grandfather. He preferred to stay indoors! On his way home one day, Cyril realized that he had lost his keys. "Where did I have them last?" he sighed. Puzzled, he retraced his steps.

He walked backwards to all the places he'd been that morning. Backwards over the wooden bridge, reversing up the maple tree and along its branches, somersaulting down into Charlie's clothes line with a backwards leap to the ground like a gymnast, and backwards up the hill to where he started. "That was fun!" he thought. He rummaged in a pile of leaves and spied his keys down a hole! It turns out Cyril is quite adventurous after all. When he got home, he made a fabric Cyril key ring so he wouldn't have to retrace his steps ever again!

You could also try:
- a tree key ring
- a banana key ring
- a leaf key ring

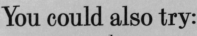

21

1

Draw a shape on card that's slightly larger than your head, with two domes for ears. Add eyes. Cut out the mask, making sure you can see out of the eye holes.

Big Ted and Wilbur's festival mask

It's party time again and Big Ted and Wilbur are having a fancy dress party. All the guests must come wearing a disguise. Here is the mask Big Ted made.

2

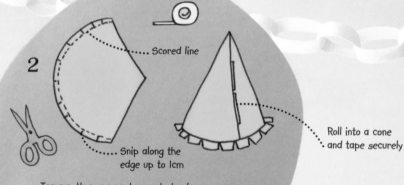

Scored line

Roll into a cone and tape securely

Snip along the edge up to 1cm

Trace the nose template (see page 48) on to card. Score a line 1cm in from the curved edge and snip along the edge. Roll the card into a cone and secure with tape.

What you will need
• card • pencil • scissors • tracing paper •
• sticky tape • crêpe paper •
• glue • elastic •

3

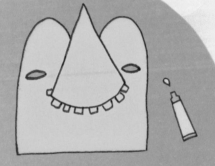

Fold out all the snipped edges to make tabs. Place the nose cone in the centre of the mask. Secure the tabs on to the mask with glue or sticky tape.

For a simpler version, you can paint or draw on your mask instead of using lots of coloured paper.

4

Scalloped edges - cut one edge of each strip into a line of small domes ....

Cut about 20 strips from two colours of crêpe paper. Shape one edge of each strip to make scalloped edges.

5

Glue a card strip over the eye holes. Cut eye holes on the strip. Then, on the bottom of the mask, stick a strip of crêpe paper. Add more strips above, each overlapping the strip below.

How about...?
See if you can make different masks for your friends. Maybe some can have card hair, triangular ears or even big, sharp teeth?

Make sure the pierced holes aren't too close to the edge of the mask ....

6

...Whiskers made from thin card strips

Cut thin card whiskers and glue them to either side of the nose. Pierce a small hole on either side of the cardboard strip on the mask. Thread and knot the elastic so the mask fits securely. You're now in disguise!

23

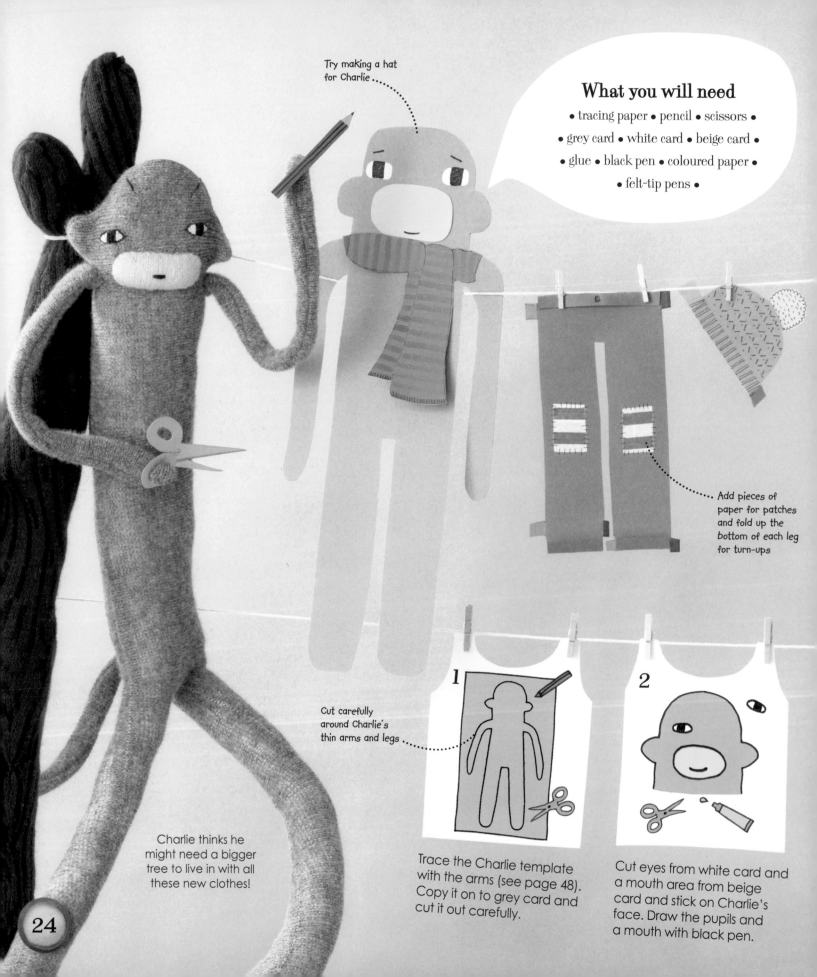

Try making a hat
for Charlie

What you will need
- tracing paper • pencil • scissors •
- grey card • white card • beige card •
- glue • black pen • coloured paper •
- felt-tip pens •

Add pieces of
paper for patches
and fold up the
bottom of each leg
for turn-ups

Cut carefully
around Charlie's
thin arms and legs

Charlie thinks he
might need a bigger
tree to live in with all
these new clothes!

24

1

Trace the Charlie template
with the arms (see page 48).
Copy it on to grey card and
cut it out carefully.

2

Cut eyes from white card and
a mouth area from beige
card and stick on Charlie's
face. Draw the pupils and
a mouth with black pen.

Charlie's clothes line

What to wear today? Charlie always likes choosing his wardrobe. His favourite outfit is his banana pyjamas! Make him paper clothes and see how they fit.

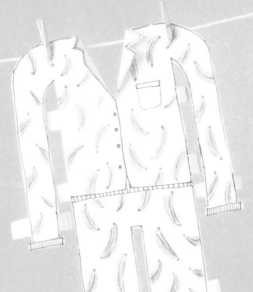

Socks have flaps at the sides and bottom

Create different patterns with felt-tip pens

How about...?

Here is a selection of Charlie's wardrobe, but what about making him shorts or a T-shirt with a banana picture on the front?

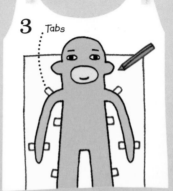

3 Tabs

Draw eyebrows above Charlie's eyes. Lay Charlie on coloured paper. For pyjamas, draw around his body and add tabs as shown.

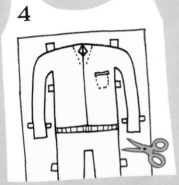

4

Lift Charlie off the paper and join up the missing bits, such as the neck line. Cut out carefully. Remember not to cut off the tabs!

5

Fold over the tabs and hook over Charlie's body. You can decorate his pyjamas with felt-tip pens. While he's asleep, make him more clothes!

Cyril's creature key ring

Cyril Squirrel-fox was always losing his keys. One day he decided to make a large, brightly coloured key ring so he would be able to find them anywhere.

With such a bright colour felt, this Cyril key ring is not going to be lost in your bag or pocket.

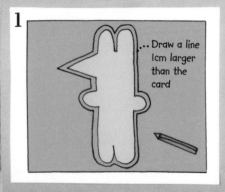

1
... Draw a line 1cm larger than the card

Trace the Cyril key ring template (see page 48) on to thick card. Cut it out. Draw around it on to felt, then draw a line 1cm larger all round.

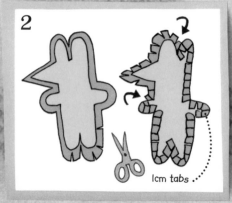

2
1cm tabs ...

Cut out the felt shape along the larger line. Snip 1cm tabs along the edge. Fold over the tabs on to the card Cyril and glue them down on to the card.

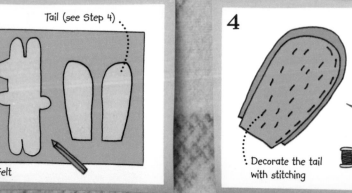

3
Tail (see Step 4)
Felt

4
Decorate the tail with stitching

How about...?
You could stuff the felt shape the way we make the Cyril doll on pages 34–35.

On more orange felt, draw around Cyril again. Cut out this Cyril shape so it's slightly smaller than the other Cyril shape.

Trace the tail template (see page 48) on to card. Cut it out and draw around it twice on to orange felt. Cut out both tails and stitch together.

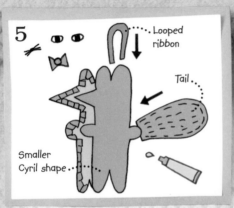

5

Looped ribbon

Tail

Smaller Cyril shape

Using strong glue, attach the tail on to the card of the first Cyril shape. Glue a piece of looped ribbon on to the card at the top. Stick the smaller Cyril shape on to the back, over the ribbon and the tail. Add thread whiskers, felt eyes and a felt bow-tie. Now you just need some keys!

The other creatures are going to be jealous of such a unique key ring!

Embroider stitching on to the tail

The felt should be smoothed on to the surface of the card

27

Ralf and Rill's draught excluder

In Ralf and Rill's house, the wind gusts through a big gap under the door. A sausage dog will stop those draughts.

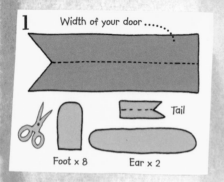

1 Width of your door ......

Foot x 8   Ear x 2   Tail

Cut a rectangle of fabric the width of your door for the sausage dog's body. Fold down the middle and cut a diagonal line for a pointy nose. Cut eight identical foot shapes, two tail shapes and two ear shapes from fabric.

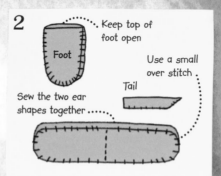

2 Keep top of foot open

Foot

Sew the two ear shapes together ......

Tail   Use a small over stitch

Sew together the two ears using an over stitch all the way round. Sew the tail in the same way. Sew two of the feet shapes together, leaving the top end open. Repeat for all four feet.

Sausage dogs are excellent at stopping a breeze under doors or windows.

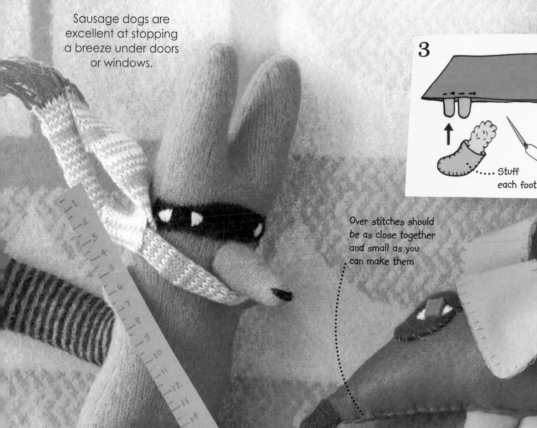

3

Stuff each foot

Stuff each of the four feet. Insert the feet and tail between the folds of the body fabric, as shown, and pin.

Over stitches should be as close together and small as you can make them

Cut a slit on the fold on the top of the head. Fold the ear piece in half and push the centre into the slit. Stitch into place.

Stitch together all the open sides of the dog's body using an over stitch, leaving a gap in the middle for the stuffing. Stuff the dog as full as you can so he's solid and stiff, then sew up the gap.

What you will need

• measuring tape • fabric • scissors •
• needle and thread • stuffing (polyester stuffing or old fabric) •
• pins • felt •

4 Push centre of ear into the top of the head

5 ..... Stuffing

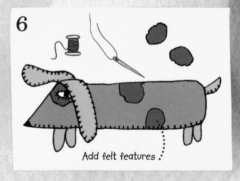

6 Add felt features

Add eyes and nose with felt shapes. If you're feeling adventurous, sew on some felt spots! Your dog is ready to stop those draughts!

Mitten Kitten's glove puppet

The musical performance was given by Wilbur the glove puppet. Everyone enjoyed the show!

Paint a backdrop to your theatrical scene or use a patterned blanket.

Try making different glove puppets to create a cast of characters.

Your thumb and little finger will move Wilbur's arms

What you will need
• grey felt • pins • black marker pen •
• scissors • needle and thread • white felt •
• black pipe cleaner • cotton wool balls •
• glue • pink felt •

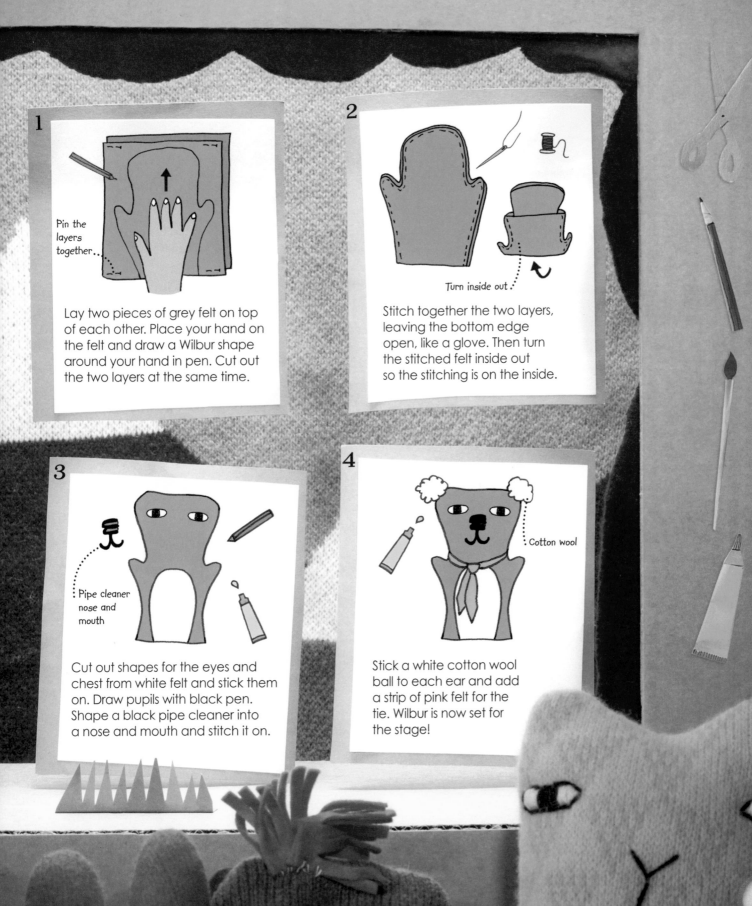

1

Pin the layers together..

Lay two pieces of grey felt on top of each other. Place your hand on the felt and draw a Wilbur shape around your hand in pen. Cut out the two layers at the same time.

2

Turn inside out..

Stitch together the two layers, leaving the bottom edge open, like a glove. Then turn the stitched felt inside out so the stitching is on the inside.

3

Pipe cleaner nose and mouth

Cut out shapes for the eyes and chest from white felt and stick them on. Draw pupils with black pen. Shape a black pipe cleaner into a nose and mouth and stitch it on.

4

Cotton wool

Stick a white cotton wool ball to each ear and add a strip of pink felt for the tie. Wilbur is now set for the stage!

31

You can make a stage from a cardboard box with a hole cut out of the front.

Mitten Kitten's finger puppets

The second act introduced two little bears and a cat made out of card. Mitten Kitten can fit them on her paws.

What you will need
- card • scissors • ruler • black pen •
- double-sided sticky tape •
- ordinary sticky tape •

Features are drawn on by pen.

This puppet has triangular ears and a tail stuck on the back of its body.

How about...?
Make a range of puppets for your fingers: rabbits, robots and maybe a monster.

1

Bumps for ears

Cut a rectangle of card about 3cm long and 4cm high. Draw a line across 1cm down from the top, making two bumps for the puppet's ears. Cut along the line.

2

Roll into a tube and tape securely

Roll the card around your finger to form a tube that fits snugly. Stick down the overlapping edge with double-sided sticky tape.

3

Arms on one piece of card, a paw at each end

Chest

Eyes x 2

Nose and mouth

For the arms, nose, chest and eyes, cut out shapes from card. With a black pen, draw paws on the arms, pupils on the eyes, a nose and mouth, and hair on the chest.

4

Stick arms to the back

Stick the arms on to the back of the finger puppet with sticky tape. Stick on the remaining features with double-sided sticky tape. Let the play begin!

Olive Owl makes Cyril

On a midnight flight through the forest, Olive was surprised to meet Cyril strolling amongst the trees. He gave Olive the idea to make a Cyril doll once she'd flown home.

1

Pin the fabric together

Reverse of fabric should be on the outside ......

Front side of fabric faces inside

Layer two fabric pieces. Trace the Cyril template (see page 48) on to card. Cut out and draw around the shapes on to the fabric.

2

Gap for stuffing ......

Gap for stuffing ......

Stitch around the drawn lines with a running stitch. Leave a 3cm gap on both the body and the tail for stuffing.

3

.... 1cm gap

Cut out your shapes, leaving a 1cm gap between the edge of the cut and the stitched line. Turn your shapes inside out. Poke out the ears and feet with a pen.

What you will need
- fabric • pins • tracing paper •
- pencil • card • scissors •
- needle and black and white thread •
- pen • polyester toy stuffing •

4

Sew the gap closed after stuffing

Use black thread to embroider lines of chest hair

Stuff the tail and body

Stuff each shape through the gaps. Sew the gap on the body closed. Embroider the eyes and nose.

5

Bottom of tail

Sew tail on to Cyril's back

Fold in the edge of the tail and stitch it on to the back of your Cyril doll. Your Cyril is ready for a forest stroll (but this time in the daylight)!

Charlie's food party

Cyril

Charlie was hungry! He was planning a surprise party for Cyril and wished to make it extra special. "What could I use to make the decorations?" he wondered. He looked around him for ideas. "Hmm, we need something bright," he said to himself as he searched... all he could see were bananas! Charlie's favourite food is banana, and he always has lots in his cupboard. "I've got it!" he exclaimed. "Banana bunting! Cyril will love it!"

He set to work with yellow card and a ribbon, and soon he had a long line of bananas to hang.

It was spectacular! The first guest was Ralf, who made a few wriggly worms (his favourite food) to add to the bunting. Then Wilbur arrived and made some green leaves. Each new guest added a favourite food, which made Charlie even more hungry!

Eventually Cyril appeared. "Surprise!" everyone shouted. Cyril was so happy with his party and the bunting decorations, and Charlie was very glad that he could start eating.

Charlie

36

Olive

Olive Owl loved the evenings. Just as it was getting dark one day, she flew up through the trees. The wind was in her wings and there were lots of clouds in the sky. She saw Mitten Kitten in a tree and swooped down. "Hello Olive, it's going to be stormy tonight!" shouted Mitten. "Maybe you should get some shelter." "I'm not afraid of a drop of rain," Olive replied, and flew as high as she could. Then there was a rumble of thunder... and a HUGE bolt of lightning shot down, narrowly missing Olive. "Phew, that was close!" she thought. "I nearly lost a tail feather!" A little shaken, Olive returned to the tree.

"Are you all right?" asked Mitten Kitten. "Yes! I had no idea storms could be so fierce!" replied Olive. That night, Olive Owl made a mobile to give to Mitten Kitten as a thank you for the warning. She made it shaped like a big rain cloud, but at least this one wasn't dangerous!

You could also try:
- a sun mobile
- a snow mobile
- a lightning mobile

Mitten Kitten

Olive's night flight

Charlie's banana bunting

Feeling hungry? Help Charlie Monkey make his friends a bunting of paper bananas to hang up in the house.

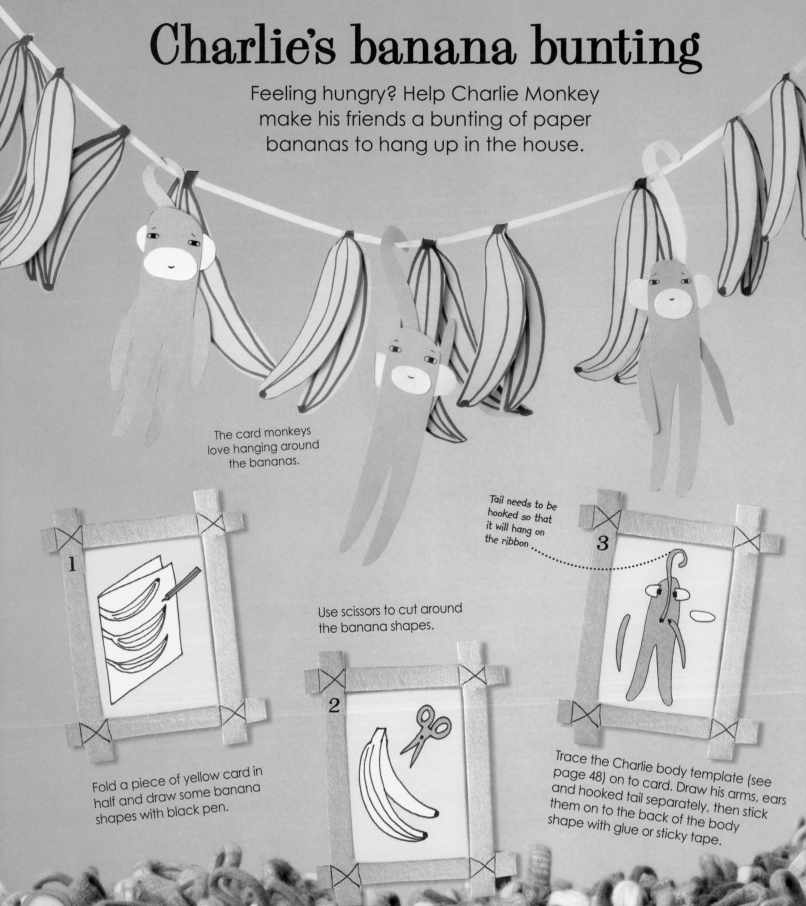

The card monkeys love hanging around the bananas.

1 Fold a piece of yellow card in half and draw some banana shapes with black pen.

Use scissors to cut around the banana shapes.

2

Tail needs to be hooked so that it will hang on the ribbon

3 Trace the Charlie body template (see page 48) on to card. Draw his arms, ears and hooked tail separately, then stick them on to the back of the body shape with glue or sticky tape.

What you will need
• yellow card • black pen • scissors •
• grey card • tracing paper • pencil • glue or
sticky tape • ribbon (3m long) •

Draw on eyes and a smile with black pen to give your monkey his very own expression.

4

Hook your bananas over the ribbon, securing them with glue or sticky tape, and hang the monkeys between them. Tie either side of the ribbon to a fence or wall so the bunting hangs. Now you can party!

5

You could make other shapes to hang on your bunting. What's your favourite food?

39

Ralf and Rill's slide and climb game

Ralf and Rill love playing games.
Sometimes they make up their own.
This one is their version of snakes
and ladders.

1 Using a ruler, draw a square 30cm x 30cm. Mark out intervals of 3cm around the edges. Join up the lines lightly in pencil to form a grid. Cut out fifty 3cm squares from different coloured card.

30cm
30cm
3cm

2 Stick the coloured squares on to every second square. Number each square in the grid from 1 to 100, starting at the bottom-right corner.

Make your own creature counters

Place the bananas and trees across the board

97. 96. 95. 84.
92. 93. 86. 76.
91. 89. 87. 75.
90. 72. 74. 65.
71. 68. 67. 66.
69. 55.
70. 53. 54.
52. 46.
51. 48. 45.
49. 35.
50. 34.
33. 26.
30. 27.
29. 28. 15.
12. 14.
11. 7.
8.
9.
10.

100

1

What you will need

• coloured card • ruler •
• pencil • scissors • glue • pen •
• green paper • yellow paper • dice •

3

Add details in pen ⋯⋯

Cut out trees from green paper and bananas from yellow paper. Make them different lengths from 5cm to 14cm. In the game, your counter climbs the trees and slides down the bananas.

4

Slide down bananas ⋯⋯

Climb trees ⋯⋯

Stick the trees and bananas so the top and bottom of each are in the middle of two squares. Space them evenly on the board. Think where they will work best.

5

Fold the tab to make the counter stand ⋯⋯

Make some friendly counters from coloured card. Cut out shapes with a rectangular tab at the bottom. Add features to your counters, fold the tabs, find a dice and start to play!

Rules of the game:
Throw the dice. Move your counter the number of squares shown on the dice. If a tree trunk is in the square you land in, climb to the square at the tree's top. If you land on a square with the top of a banana, slide down the banana. The first to reach 100 wins.

Big Ted and Wilbur's robot

What a mess – empty cartons and bits of paper everywhere! Big Ted and Wilbur make a robot to help them reuse old boxes and tidy up.

1 Tabs ...   Fold down tabs ...

Snip around the top of two toilet roll tubes to make tabs. Fold down the tabs and stick them to the underside of the larger cardboard box to make legs.

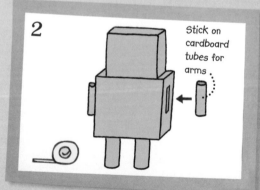

2   Stick on cardboard tubes for arms ...

Stick the smaller cardboard box on to the larger box. Stick the side of each cardboard tube arm to either side of the box with double-sided sticky tape or glue.

This robot is one example of what you can do with old packaging. See what you can create with what you can find around you.

What you will need

- five cardboard tubes •
- scissors • two cardboard boxes •
- card packaging • glue or double-sided sticky tape • foil • felt-tip pens •

Perhaps make card tools for your robot.

42

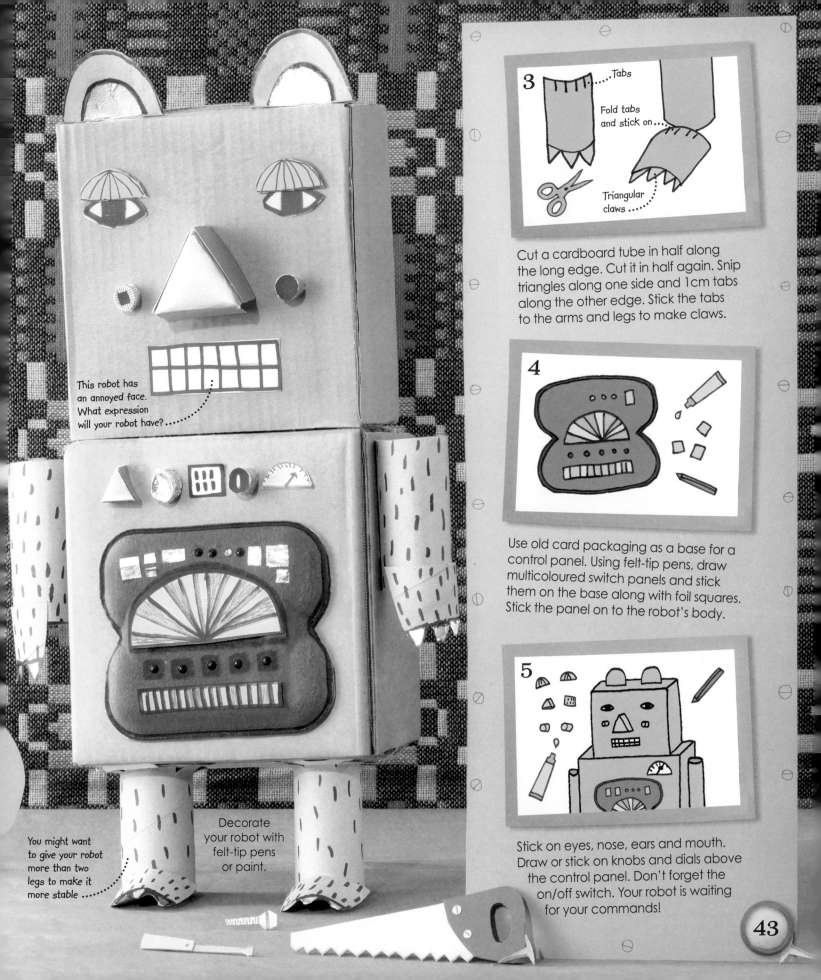

This robot has an annoyed face. What expression will your robot have? .....

You might want to give your robot more than two legs to make it more stable .....

Decorate your robot with felt-tip pens or paint.

3

.....Tabs

Fold tabs and stick on.....

Triangular claws .....

Cut a cardboard tube in half along the long edge. Cut it in half again. Snip triangles along one side and 1cm tabs along the other edge. Stick the tabs to the arms and legs to make claws.

4

Use old card packaging as a base for a control panel. Using felt-tip pens, draw multicoloured switch panels and stick them on the base along with foil squares. Stick the panel on to the robot's body.

5

Stick on eyes, nose, ears and mouth. Draw or stick on knobs and dials above the control panel. Don't forget the on/off switch. Your robot is waiting for your commands!

Cyril makes Charlie

Cyril Squirrel-fox shows you how to make your own sleeping Charlie, but "Ssshhhhh" – you don't want to wake him!

If you want an awake Charlie, add wide-open eyes instead – two ovals of white felt with embroidered black pupils. Or maybe he could be winking?

Make your Charlie doll some bedroom furniture from cardboard.

1

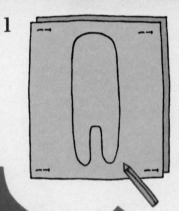

Lay two pieces of felt on top of each other. Pin together. Trace the Charlie body template (see page 48) on to card. Cut out the shape and draw around it on the felt.

2 Stitch over the lines on the Charlie doll body and leave a 3cm gap in the side for stuffing. Cut out the shape, leaving a 1cm gap between the edge and the stitching. Turn the shape inside out, stuff and stitch the stuffing gap closed.

Add stuffing through the 3cm gap

Use a pencil to poke out the legs when turning inside out

3

Add a pink paw to the end of each arm.

Roll up each felt rectangle

For the arms and the tail, trace the templates (see page 48) on to grey felt. Cut out and roll. Stitch the long edges closed so they won't unroll. Make paws from pink felt and stitch them on to the arms.

4

Ear

Mouth

Cut out an oval shape from beige felt and two pink ears. Stitch the ears on to the sides of the head and stitch or glue on the oval between the ears. Embroider a mouth and closed eyes.

5

Stitch arms to each side of Charlie's body using an over stitch. Stitch the tail on to the back of the body, just above the legs. Your Charlie doll is ready to take a nap!

Tail

Z Z Z z z ᶻ

What you will need
• grey felt • pins • tracing paper •
• pencil • card • scissors • needle and thread •
• polyester toy stuffing •
• pink felt • beige felt •

45

Olive Owl's cloud mobile

Olive loves flying around the night skies, especially when it's cool and cloudy. Make a fabric cloud mobile for Olive to fly around in.

Olive Owl's feathers keep her cosy and warm when she's flying.

Your owl can be any colour you like. Use a different colour for the beak and feet. You and around the eyes. You could even use old, patterned fabric.

What you will need

- two layers of felt or fabric
- black pen • needle and thread
- scissors • stuffing • ribbon

Try pinning the two layers together to stop them moving

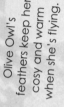

1

Lay two layers of felt or fabric with front sides against each other. Mark out a cloud, several raindrop shapes and an owl shape with black pen.

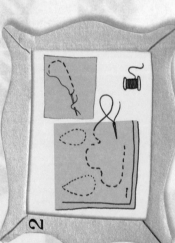

2

Using a needle and thread, sew a short running stitch around your marked lines, remembering to leave a gap in each shape to help you turn it inside out.

How about...?
Your owl doesn't have to fly in the rain. Try making a sun mobile with white clouds hanging from it. Or a grey cloud with snow falling from it.

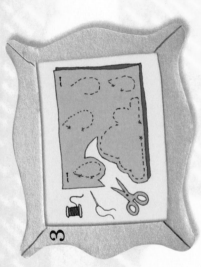

3

Cut around the outside of each shape, about 1cm from the stitching.

4

Push out all the pointy areas with a pencil...

Turn your shapes inside out through the gap in each one. Push stuffing into each gap until the shapes are filled, feeling firm and three-dimensional.

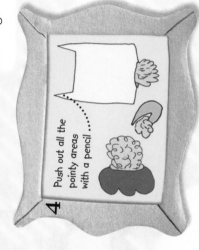

5

Gap has been stitched...

Neatly stitch up the gaps in each shape to close in the stuffing. Sew lengths of ribbons on the tip of the raindrops and the top of the owl's head.

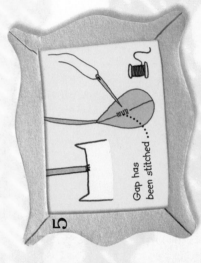

6

Stitch V-shaped marks here to look like feathers

7

Decorate your owl by cutting out a beak, two feet and a pair of wings from different colours of fabric or felt. Make your own design to make your owl unique.

Attach the raindrops and owl to the bottom of the cloud with several layers of stitching. Sew a ribbon to the top of the cloud to hang it with. Let your mobile catch the breeze.

Templates

These templates will help you make some of the creatures. You need to trace them.

How to trace: Lay tracing paper over the template and draw over the line with a soft, dark pencil. Turn over the tracing paper and retrace over the line on the other side. Flip the tracing paper the right way up again and lay it on a piece of card or paper. Draw over the line, pressing down quite hard, so that the pencil lines from the back of your tracing marks the card, leaving a copy of the shape.

You will find the Charlie Monkey template at the very front of the book.

Page 44 - trace the body without the arms; trace the rectangular arm (centre) twice and the tail (bottom)

The template for the nose cone and Cyril Squirrel-fox key ring are on the opposite page.

The Cyril Squirrel-fox doll template is at the very back of the book.

Page 38 - trace tail

Page 24 - trace the body with arms attached

Page 38 - trace the body without ears and arms; trace the arms separately following the dotted lines

Trace this nose cone for the pop-up card on page 13 and the festival mask on page 22

Trace these body and tail templates for the Cyril Key ring on page 26

48

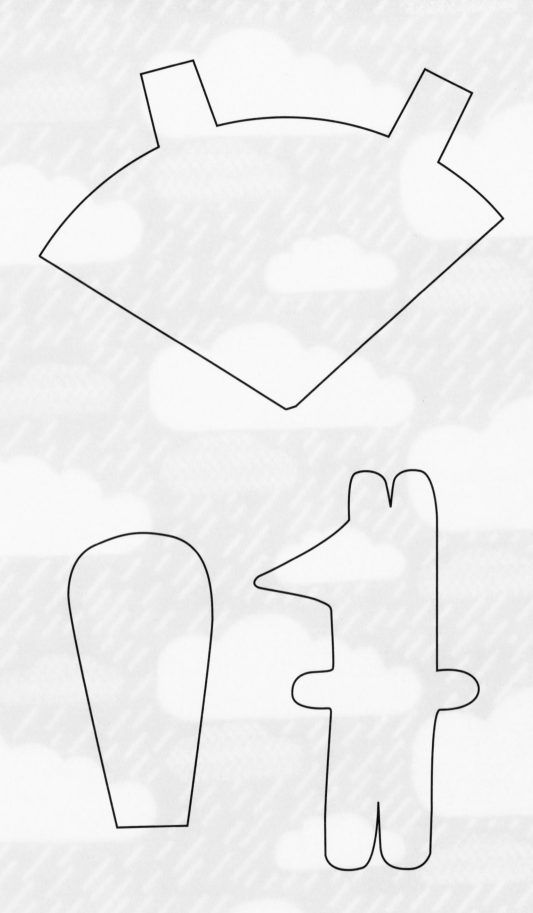